D0307003

497 442 87 3

GREATEST WARRIORS
ROMAN SOLDIERS

PETER HEPPLEWHITE

FRANKLIN WATTS
LONDON · SYDNEY

First published in 2013 by Franklin Watts

Copyright © 2013 Arcturus Publishing Limited

Franklin Watts
338 Euston Road
London
NW1 3BH

Franklin Watts Australia
Level 17/207 Kent Street, Sydney, NSW 2000

Produced by Arcturus Publishing Limited,
26/27 Bickels Yard, 151–153 Bermondsey Street, London SE1 3HA

All rights reserved.

Edited and designed by: Discovery Books Ltd.

Series concept: Joe Harris
Managing editor for Discovery Books: Laura Durman
Editor: Clare Collinson
Picture researcher: Clare Collinson
Designer: Ian Winton

The publisher would like to thank the following re-enactment groups for their assistance in the preparation of this book: Britannia (www.durolitum.co.uk/) and Ermine Street Guard (http://www.erminestreetguard.co.uk/).
Picture credits:
Alamy: pp. 4, 28 (Photos 12), p. 7 (INTERFOTO), pp. 14, 15, 16 (Stephen Mulcahey), p. 18 (Jeff Morgan 16), p. 26 (AF archive), p. 27 (Martin Jenkinson); Britannia (www.durolitum.co.uk/): p. 22; Ermine Street Guard: pp. 9, 19tr; Getty Images: p. 6 (Celia Paterson), p. 21 (Gamma-Rapho), p. 23 (uplifted); Shutterstock Images: p. 10l (greglith), p. 10r (Rolandino), p. 17 (Regien Paassen), p. 24 (McCarthy's PhotoWorks), p. 29 (StockPhotoAstur); Wikimedia Commons: pp. title, 5, 11l, 11r, 12, 19bl, 25 (MatthiasKabel), p. 8 (Luc Viatour), p. 13, p. 20 (Portable Antiquities Scheme).
Cover images: Shutterstock Images: top (SueC), bottom centre (meunierd), background (Francisco Javier Gil).

A CIP record for this book is available from the British Library

Dewey Decimal Classification Number: 355.1'0937

ISBN 978 1 4451 1863 5

Franklin Watts is a division of Hachette Children's Books, an Hachette UK company.
www.hachette.co.uk

Printed in China

SL002668EN
Supplier 03, Date 0513, Print Run 2359

CONTENTS

The Roman army was the greatest fighting force in the ancient world. It conquered and defended a vast **empire** that lasted for over 500 years (27 BCE–476 CE). Roman warriors were highly trained, tightly disciplined and well armed. Battle **tactics**, practised over and over again, made Roman soldiers very hard to beat.

SUPREME WARRIORS

The most important soldiers in the Roman army were infantry, or foot soldiers. They served in units called legions, each with around 5,000 men.

A PROFESSIONAL ARMY

By the first century CE, Rome's empire covered most of Europe, North Africa and the Middle East. To conquer new lands and defend its **frontiers**, Rome built up a permanent army, made up of professional, full-time soldiers. Ruthless and highly skilled in battle, Roman **legionaries** were the most powerful and feared warriors of their time.

CAVALRY

Every legion had a small force of about 120 cavalry, or soldiers who fought on horseback.

COMBAT STATS

Empire and army, 117 CE

- **Population of Rome:** around 1 million
- **Population of the Roman Empire:** around 88 million
- **Size of Roman Empire:** 6.5 million sq km (2.5 million sq mi)
- **Number of troops:** about 350,000 (legionaries and **auxiliaries**)
- **Long-lasting legion:** Third Cyrenean Legion - by 117 CE, it had already existed for over 150 years and continued to fight for another 350 years

CRACK TROOPS

Roman legionaries were the most disciplined and well-organized warriors the world had ever known. They received rigorous training and obeyed commands without question and without delay. On the battlefield, they fought as units, forming a fearsome war machine.

ROUTE MARCH

Legionaries were trained to march quickly. Three times a month every legion underwent a gruelling route march in full armour – 35 km (22 mi) in 5 hours at a quick step.

CITIZEN ARMY

The legionaries in the **imperial** army were all Roman **citizens** – free men who could vote in elections. They were mainly volunteers who served 20 years as full-time soldiers, followed by five years as **reserves**. They received 225 *denarii* a year for their service and a pension of 3,000 *denarii* or a grant of land when they retired.

FIGHTING UNITS

The number of legions in the army varied, but it was usually around 30.
Each soldier belonged to a squad called a *contubernia*, a group of eight men
who shared a tent and ate together. Ten *contubernia* made up a **century**. Six
centuries made up a **cohort** and there were 10 cohorts in each legion.

MASTERS OF MOVEMENT

Roman legionaries were trained to manoeuvre with
great precision and organization. The units formed a
close-knit fighting force that seemed unstoppable.

COMBAT STATS

Imperial legions

- **Legions:** around 30 legions in the Roman army, each
  with about 5,000 men
- **Cohorts:** 10 cohorts in each legion; 9 cohorts with
  480 men and 1 cohort with 800 men
- **Centuries:** 6 centuries of 80 men in each cohort,
  except the first cohort, which had 5 double-strength
  centuries of 160 men
- **Contubernia:** 10 *contubernia* of 8 men in each century

OFFICERS IN COMMAND

Roman legionaries were the supreme warriors of their day, but key to their success were the officers in charge. The commanding officer of each legion was the legate. He was hand-picked by the **emperor** and usually a **noble** and a **senator**. But the **centurions** were the backbone of the army. They led the soldiers into battle.

TRANSVERSE CREST

A centurion's helmet had a large plumed crest running from ear to ear, so his men could see him in battle.

CENTURION

A centurion was the officer in charge of each century.

MILITARY MEDALS

Military awards or medals, called *phalerae*, were worn on the centurion's chest.

SPECIAL DUTIES

Second in command of each century was the *optio*. He helped to organize the troops and ensured that the centurion's orders were carried out. Each century also included officers with special duties.

VEXILLARIUS

The *vexillarius* was the officer who carried the flag of the legion, the *vexillum*.

OPTIO

The *optio's* badge of office was a decorated silver staff.

CORNICEN

The trumpet blower, or *cornicen*, helped soldiers march in time and give signals to the troops. When battle noise drowned the commands of officers, a trumpet blast meant 'look at the standard and follow it'. *Cornicens* wore a wolf skin as part of their uniform.

SIGNIFER

Each century had a **standard** bearer called a *signifer*. The standard bearer could pass on simple orders, such as 'advance', by raising, lowering or waving the standard.

FIGHTING TALK

Verus – ambitious centurion

Verus was an able centurion who became a senator and commander of the Third Gallic Legion in Syria. But in 219 CE he became too ambitious. He led his legion in a rebellion against Emperor Elagabalus and proclaimed himself emperor. As punishment, Verus was executed and the legion was broken up – a great disgrace.

EQUIPPED FOR CONQUEST

Roman soldiers were highly skilled with a variety of deadly weapons. A legionary's main armaments were his sword, shield and javelin. He could also call on other weapons, such as daggers and darts, when the need arose.

JAVELIN

A legionary's javelin (*pilum*) was a 2-m (6.6-ft) long wooden shaft with a barbed iron tip for piercing armour. Javelins could be used in hand-to-hand combat but were usually thrown before engaging with the enemy. They had a maximum range of about 30 m (100 ft).

SWORD

A Roman legionary's most important weapon was his sword (*gladius*). This was made of double-edged steel, strengthened with carbon.

SHIELD

The curved, rectangular Roman shield was called a *scutum*. It was not just used for defence. In close combat, a legionary would ram his opponent with the shield, while thrusting with his sword.

A WARRIOR'S KIT

In early Roman times, mules were used to carry most of a legionary's equipment. But large baggage trains slowed armies down, so from the 1st century BCE legionaries were expected to carry as much of their own equipment as they could. Each soldier also had to carry his share of the tools, such as spades, axes and picks, that would be needed for building camps and fortifications at the end of the march.

HEAVY LOAD

As well as their own weapons and armour, Roman legionaries on the march had to carry a heavy kit pack on a wooden cross frame.

MARCHING PACK

A legionary's pack included between three and 15 days' worth of food supplies, as well as pans for cooking and a bedroll or cloak.

COMBAT STATS

Equipment stats

- **Length of sword:** 64-81 cm (25-32 in)
- **Length of dagger:** 20-25 cm (8-10 in)
- **Length of spear:** about 2 m (6.6 ft)
- **Total weight of equipment carried:** at least 27 kg (60 lb) - about the weight of a husky dog!

DRESSED FOR WAR

Roman legionaries fought many vicious battles throughout the empire. To protect themselves from their enemies' weapons they wore the best armour in the ancient world.

MAIL ARMOUR

Chain mail armour was used throughout the Roman period. The mail was made by linking thousands of small iron rings together.

SHIELD

As well as body armour, a legionary had a shield for protection against enemy blows. Shaped to curve around the body, it was about 120 cm (4 ft) long and 60 cm (2 ft) wide. It weighed about 10 kg (22 lb).

GREAVES

Leg armour called 'greaves' gave protection from the knee to the ankle. In later times, only centurions wore greaves.

SANDALS

A legionary's sandals were designed to help him march for long distances. They were strong and well ventilated and often had metal studs on the soles to make them last longer.

PLATE ARMOUR

Chain mail armour could withstand cuts from swords, but did not give good protection from stabbing blows. From the 1st century CE, legionaries wore armour made of curved plates, called *lorica segmentata*. This gave excellent protection for the body and shoulders.

HELMET

Helmets of brass or iron protected the head. Hinged cheek plates were tied with leather straps under the chin. The helmets were designed to allow for good vision and hearing. A guard, sticking out from the back, protected the soldier's neck.

OVERLAPPING ARMOUR

Lorica segmentata was body armour made from overlapping metal strips held together with hinges and leather straps. This not only gave the wearer protection, but also freedom of movement.

FIGHTING TALK

Uniform protection

Roman legionaries wore a standard uniform, depending on their unit. This meant items such as helmets or sandals could be made in large numbers to keep costs down. Soldiers had to pay for any lost or damaged kit, so it was usually well looked after.

BACK-UP TROOPS

Roman legions were given vital support by auxiliaries. Auxiliaries were light infantry or cavalry, and included troops with specialist skills. They had an important role to play in battle, often joining the legionaries at the forefront of the fighting.

CAVALRY

Every Roman legion included a small number of cavalry, but auxiliaries provided most of the cavalry in the Roman army. They were recruited from tribes around the empire that were skilled in horsemanship.

SHIELD

Auxiliary cavalry carried flat shields that were oval, rectangular or hexagonal.

SPECIAL FORCES

Unlike legionaries, auxiliaries were not Roman citizens. They were soldiers recruited from the lands that Rome had conquered. They helped to defend the empire's borders and brought a range of different fighting skills to the battlefield. After 25 years of service they were rewarded with the prize of citizenship.

ARCHERS

The best Roman archers came from Crete and Syria. They used bows made from layers of sinew, wood and horn glued together.

ARMOUR

Auxiliaries often wore chain mail shirts over a tunic. Their helmets were similar to those of legionaries.

COMBAT STATS

Auxiliary forces

The Roman imperial army included around 200,000 auxiliaries. They were divided into units containing:

- **Cavalry:** 40 troops of horsemen, each with 32 men (40 x 32 = 1,280 soldiers)
- **Infantry:** 16 centuries, each with 80 men (16 x 80 = 1,280 men)
- **Mixed forces:** 6 centuries of 80 infantry (6 x 80 = 480 men) working with 4 cavalry troops

FIGHTING AS A UNIT

Roman armies won battles because they fought together as units of highly trained soldiers working in **formation**. They used a range of battle tactics, depending on the circumstances. Careful planning, flexibility and discipline were key to their success.

BATTLE LINES

In battle, legionaries moved forwards in lines. Their shields formed a defensive wall against oncoming weapons. When soldiers in the front line became exhausted, they moved back and soldiers in the line behind took their place.

TESTUDO FORMATION

The tortoise, or testudo, formation was used for attacking forts or against mounted archers. The soldiers at the front interlocked their upright shields. The soldiers behind raised their shields above their heads to form a protective 'shell'. This shell was so strong that, in training, a chariot could be driven across the top.

FIGHTING TALK

Battlefield commands

ad aciem: form battle line (ranks facing the enemy)

pila iacite: throw javelins

cuneum facite: form a wedge (an attack formation to break enemy lines)

gladios stringite: draw swords

parate: get ready to charge

percutite: charge

testudinem facite: form testudo

FIREPOWER

As well as swords and spears, Roman warriors used heavy weapons, or artillery, on the battlefield, including catapults that fired a range of devastating missiles. When they attacked an enemy fortress or city, Roman soldiers used **catapults** and **ballistas**, supported by **battering rams** and high **siege towers**.

DEADLY ONAGER

The most fearsome and powerful Roman catapult was the onager. It got its name from a type of wild ass (the onager), because of the way it kicked when fired.

SLING

A sling attached to the firing arm held the missiles, perhaps one large rock or a barrage of smaller stones.

FIRING ARM

A long wooden arm was fastened with thick, twisted ropes that acted like springs. Soldiers pulled back the arm with a **winch**, twisting the ropes tighter. When the arm was released it shot forwards, firing rocks to smash through stone walls.

WAR MACHINES

Every Roman legion was equipped with a variety of powerful artillery weapons. The artillery men were called *ballistarii* – and they dreaded wet weather. If rain soaked the ropes that gave the catapults their tension, or power, they were useless.

ANCIENT BALLISTA

The ballista was like a giant crossbow. Two soldiers turned winch wheels to pull the arms back and fire huge arrows at the enemy.

SCORPIO

The scorpio was a lethal weapon of great precision and power. It was designed to give a clear view of the target. It fired **bolts** that could pierce through armour and kill enemy soldiers at a distance of 100 m (110 yd).

COMBAT STATS

Legionary firepower

- **Onager:** 10 in each legion; hurled rocks weighing up to 70 kg (150 lb)
- **Ballista:** 20 in each legion; range 275-500 m (300-550 yd); speed of missile up to 184 k/ph (115 mph)
- **Scorpio:** 60 in each legion; range up to 400 m (440 yd); firing rate of up to 3-4 bolts per minute

MAKING CAMP

On **campaign**, Roman soldiers spent many days on the march. At the end of each day, they set up well-organized camps, heavily defended by ditches and lines of sharpened stakes. Tents were set up in rows – one for each squad of eight men.

MESSMATES

Recruits lived in 8-man squads called *contubernia*. A legionary's *contubernium* became like his family. The soldiers ate, slept and trained together, and fought next to one another in battle.

HEAVY EQUIPMENT

The heavy equipment needed in camp was carried by mules. This included tents and large cooking pots, as well as grind stones for making flour from the grain rations.

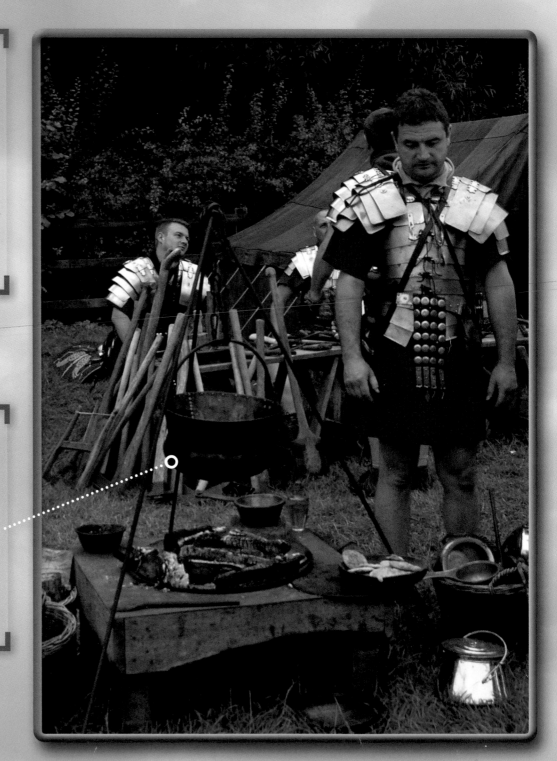

CAMP ORGANIZATION

Roman legionaries would march for around five hours a day and then stop to make camp. They were experts at setting up camp quickly and efficiently, with each soldier having specific duties. Camps varied in size, but they all had the same basic layout.

COMMANDER IN CAMP

Centurions were responsible for discipline in camp. Punishments included giving soldiers rations of hated barley instead of wheat. For serious offences, such as running away in battle, a soldier faced *fustuarium* — being beaten to death by the men whose lives he had put at risk.

TENT

The tents in this reconstructed Roman camp are made from canvas, but Roman warriors slept in tents that were usually made from calf or goat skin.

FIGHTING TALK

Rations

The Roman army didn't provide meals but issued rations, with each squad cooking their own food. Legionaries were given a daily grain ration of 1.5 kg (3 lb 5 oz). The main ration was wheat grain, made into bread or a type of porridge called *puls*. *Puls* was made with grain, water, salt and oil or milk. Spices, vegetables or bacon could be added.

FORTS AND FRONTIERS

Roman legions were not just fighting forces. Part of the job of the army was to build permanent forts and lines of defence on the borders of the empire. Legions included architects and engineers, and many soldiers were skilled craftsmen, such as stonemasons and carpenters.

CONSTRUCTION TEAM

When the Romans conquered new territory, they then had to defend it. Roman soldiers dug defensive ditches along the frontiers of the empire, as well as forts surrounded by **ramparts**.

FRONTIER DEFENDERS

The most important frontier in the empire was the Limes Germanicus. This was in Europe, along the Rhine and Danube rivers. It divided the Roman Empire from Germanic tribes. The frontier stretched for 568 km (353 mi) and there were 60 forts and 900 watchtowers along its length. Fifteen legions were stationed there.

PATROLLING HADRIAN'S WALL

The best surviving frontier is Hadrian's Wall in Britain. The mighty wall formed the northern frontier between Roman Britain and Scotland. It was guarded and patrolled by auxiliary forces for almost 250 years.

COMBAT STATS

Hadrian's Wall

- **Built:** 122-128 CE by Emperor Hadrian
- **Length:** 118 km (73 mi)
- **Height:** about 4.5 m (15 ft)
- **Thickness:** up to 3 m (10 ft)
- **Forts:** 16 large forts along the wall, each housing between 500 and 1,000 men; 79 small forts at intervals of 1,500 m (5,000 ft)

THE SACRED EAGLE

One of the most important roles in a Roman legion was that of the *aquilifer*, who carried the legion's eagle standard. The eagle was a sacred **emblem**, held high on a pole in battle so everyone could see it. It was the legion's most treasured possession and legionaries would die to protect it from capture.

AQUILA
Every legion had an eagle standard (*aquila*), displaying an eagle with outstretched wings. If the *aquila* fell into enemy hands during battle, it brought disgrace on the legion.

SPQR
The letters SPQR stood for '*senatus populusque Romanus*' ('the senate and people of Rome') – the Roman state, for which the legions were fighting.

ARMY COMMANDER
Standards often showed an image of the reigning emperor, the commander of the Roman army. This standard of the 10th Legion depicts the Emperor Tiberius (ruled 14–37 CE).

RALLYING POINT

On the march, the *aquilifer* carried the eagle standard at the front. Each century also had a standard, called a *signum*. Carried by the *signifer*, this tall standard was an important rallying point for soldiers during battle.

SIGNUM

Each century had its own unique standard, the *signum*, carried by the *signifer*.

METAL DISCS

A century's *signum* displayed up to six metal discs. The number of discs may have indicated the number of the century within the cohort to which it belonged.

BATTLE REPORT

The Battle of Carrhae, 53 BCE

At the Battle of Carrhae, in the Province of Syria (modern Turkey), Parthian horse archers and cavalry completely defeated seven Roman legions led by General Marcus Crassus. The legionary standards were captured and Rome was shamed. The standards were kept by the Parthians for 33 years, until Emperor Augustus negotiated their return in 20 BCE. This was seen as one of Augustus' great achievements.

THE GREATEST COMMANDER

Rome had many great military commanders, but most historians agree that the most brilliant Roman general was Gaius Julius Caesar. With his vast army, Caesar conquered Gaul in 58–50 BCE and invaded Britain twice, in 55 and 54 BCE.

HAIL CAESAR!
Julius Caesar (played here by Timothy Dalton in the film *Cleopatra*) was a popular and powerful general. He became dictator, or sole ruler, of the Roman Empire, before being assassinated by his enemies in Rome, in 44 BCE.

SUCCESS IN GAUL

Julius Caesar led the Roman army to victory in many great battles. One of his greatest successes was the siege of the huge hill fort of Alesia in Gaul, in 52 BCE. After a seven-year campaign, Gaul had finally been conquered.

ENCLOSING WALL

Caesar ordered his men to surround Alesia with wooden fortifications, which enclosed the Gauls in the hill fort and cut off their supplies. He hoped to starve the Gauls into surrender.

WATCHTOWER

Every 24 m (80 ft) along the walls, the Romans built a watchtower equipped with ballistas.

BATTLE REPORT

Siege of Alesia, 52 BCE

The siege of Alesia is considered a classic example of siege tactics and one of Caesar's greatest military achievements. Caesar's men built a line of fortifications 18 km (11 mi) long to trap 80,000 Gauls inside the hill fort. They then constructed another set 22 km (13 mi) long to keep out a relieving army of 60,000 soldiers. In the final battle, Caesar's army of 40,000 was close to defeat when Caesar led a surprise cavalry attack against the rear of the enemy's relief force. The retreating Gallic warriors were slaughtered or captured and every Roman soldier was given a prisoner for a slave.

END OF EMPIRE

By the end of the 3rd century CE, the mighty Roman Empire had split into two parts – the Western Empire, with its capital in Rome, and the Eastern Empire, with its capital in Byzantium, today's Istanbul. The empire in the East remained strong, but the Western Empire was crumbling. Its defences had become weak and soon it was overrun by invaders.

FACING INVASION

By the 3rd century CE, the Roman Empire was suffering wave after wave of **barbarian** invasions. Facing continual attacks on its borders, the once **invincible** Roman legions began to lose control.

FIGHTING TALK

Romans vs Goths

In 378 CE, Emperor Valens fought an army of **Goths** at Adrianople in modern Turkey. The Goths were a barbarian people who had been allowed to settle in the empire as allies, but rebelled when they were mistreated. Valens' army of around 20,000, mostly legionary infantry, was wiped out by Goth cavalry. The battle signalled the beginning of the collapse of the Western Roman Empire.

COLLAPSING EMPIRE

By the 5th century CE, invaders had swept right across the Western Empire. In 406 CE, **Vandals** took control of Gaul. In 410 CE, the last Roman soldiers pulled out of Britain, leaving the British to face fierce attacks from **Saxon** raiders. In the same year, Rome itself was captured and burned by **Visigoths**. In 476 CE, the last western emperor, Romulus Augustulus, was replaced by the barbarian general Odoacer, who declared himself King of Italy. The Western Empire had come to an end.

VANDAL ATTACK!

In the early 5th century CE, the Vandals were among the most powerful threats to the Roman legions. They moved through Gaul into Spain, set up a kingdom in North Africa, and in 455 CE they destroyed the city of Rome.

GLOSSARY

Auxiliary A soldier who provided support to the Roman legions.

Ballista A heavy weapon like a giant crossbow.

Barbarian A Roman word for non-Romans (literally 'bearded ones').

Battering ram A heavy beam used to smash down walls.

Bolt A short, heavy arrow.

Campaign A military operation in a particular area.

Centurion A commander of a century in the Roman army.

Century A unit of 80 men (originally 100) in the Roman army. The centuries in the first cohort were double-strength, with 160 men.

Citizen In Rome, a man entitled to vote in elections and serve in the legions.

Cohort A unit in the Roman army consisting of six centuries (except the first cohort in each legion, which consisted of five double-strength centuries).

Denarius A Roman coin (plural *denarii*).

Emblem A symbol.

Emperor The ruler of an empire.

Empire A country or state and all the lands it controls.

Formation In battle, the way soldiers are arranged.

Frontier The border at the edge of a country or empire.

Gaul The Roman province that covered France, Belgium and the Rhine region of Germany.

Goth A memember of a Germanic people that invaded the Roman Empire.

Imperial Relating to an empire.

Invincible Unbeatable.

Legionary A soldier serving in a Roman legion.

Noble A person belonging to the aristocratic class.

Rampart A mound of earth raised to fortify a place.

Reserves Soldiers outside the front line who were held back in case they were needed.

Saxon A member of a Germanic people that conquered parts of Britain.

Senator An official in the Roman government.

Siege A military operation in which forces try to capture a fortress, town or city.

Standard A military symbol, like a flag.

Tactic The way a plan, such as a battle plan, is carried out.

Vandal A member of a Germanic people that invaded Rome, Gaul, Spain and North Africa.

Visigoth A member of a branch of the Goths.

Winch A crank or handle.

FURTHER INFORMATION

Books

Butterfield, Moira. *Romans* (Weird True Facts). Franklin Watts, 2012.

Hewitt, Sally. *The Romans*. Franklin Watts, 2013.

Senker, Cath. *The Romans*. Wayland, 2012.

Sims, Leslie. *Roman Soldier's Handbook*. Usborne, 2009.

Steele, Philip. *Navigators: Ancient Rome*. Kingfisher, 2009.

Williams, Brian. *Life in Roman Britain*. Heinemann Library, 2010.

Woolf, Alex. *Roman Britain*. Franklin Watts, 2012.

Websites

Ermine Street Guard

www.erminestreetguard.co.uk/

The informative website of one of the oldest Roman re-enactment groups in the world, famous for recreating and testing Roman weapons and equipment.

Romans in Britain

www.romans-in-britain.org.uk

A site that gives a good introduction to Roman Britain.

The Roman Army

www.bbc.co.uk/schools/romans/army.shtml

A fun site with some great pictures.

The Roman Empire

www.roman-empire.net/index.html

A website packed with information and images.

The Roman Military Research Society

www.romanarmy.net/

The website of a research and re-enactment group, with some interesting articles.

Index

GREATEST WARRIORS

SERIES CONTENTS

GLADIATORS • Extreme entertainment • Doomed to die • Samnite – the stabber • Thracian – the slicer • *Retiarius* – the net warrior • Fighting women • Horsemen • Fight school • Amphitheatres of blood • Horror hunts • Gladiators on water • Great gladiators • Rise and fall

GREEK SOLDIERS • Greece at war • Warrior kings • All-powerful hoplites • Hoplite training • Battle armour • Weapons of war • The mighty phalanx • Warships • Citadels and sieges • Wars with Persia • Persian defeat • Alexander the Great • Greece vs Rome

KNIGHTS • Mounted warriors • Shining armour • Weapons of war • The medieval battle horse • Training a knight • Tournaments • Invasion forces • Battle • Castle strongholds • Prisoners and hostages • Civilized knights • Mythical knight: King Arthur • A new era

PIRATES • Robbers of the sea • Pirates of the Golden Age • Bloody buccaneers • Tricks and terror • Blackbeard • Armed to the teeth • Ship ahoy! • Take aim ... fire! • Attack! • Stolen treasure • Pirate women • The pirate knight • Pirates of the China Seas

ROMAN SOLDIERS • Imperial army • Crack troops • Officers in command • Equipped for conquest • Dressed for war • Back-up troops • Fighting as a unit • Firepower • Making camp • Forts and frontiers • The sacred eagle • The greatest commander • End of empire

VIKINGS • Viking raiders! • Battle ready • Weapons of war • Battle armour • Close combat • Sailing to war • Raids and plunder • Grand armies • Pitched battle • Berserk! • Warriors on the defence • Warriors of the world • Viking twilight